A DOGS LIFE

CREATIVE EDUCATION · CREATIVE PAPERBACKS

Published by Creative Education and Creative Paperbacks
P.O. Box 227, Mankato, Minnesota 56002
Creative Education and Creative Paperbacks
are imprints of The Creative Company
www.thecreativecompany.us

Design and production by Chelsey Luther
Art direction by Rita Marshall
Printed in the United States of America

Photographs by Alamy (Juniors Bildarchiv GmbH, Life on white), Dreamstime (Michael Pettigrew), Getty Images (Faba-Photography/Moment, Mint Images - Norah Levine/ Mint Images RF, Stefano Pisu/EyeEm), iStockphoto (alexei_tm, Orbon Alija, Helioscribe, Przemysław Iciak, Keyshort), Chelsey Luther, Shutterstock (Aurora72, Cerovsek Barbara, CNuisin, Emily frost, Golden Pixels LLC, petrovichli-li, Monika Vosahlova)

Library of Congress Cataloging-in-Publication Data
Names: Rosen, Michael J., author.
Title: Speaking to your dog / Michael J. Rosen.
Series: A dog's life.
Summary: An instructional guide to speaking to dogs, this title touches on how to train, praise, and speak to a dog and informs young dog owners what to expect from the loyal, loving animals.
Identifiers: ISBN 978-1-64026-057-3 (hardcover) / ISBN 978-1-62832-645-1 (pbk) / ISBN 978-1-64000-173-2 (eBook)
This title has been submitted for CIP processing under LCCN 2018938965.

CCSS: RI.1.1, 2, 4, 5, 6, 7; RI.2.1, 2, 5, 6, 7; RI.3.1, 5, 7; RF.1.1, 3, 4; RF.2.3, 4

First Edition HC 9 8 7 6 5 4 3 2 1
First Edition PBK 9 8 7 6 5 4 3 2 1

SPEAKING
to Your Dog

CONTENTS

If Your Dog Could Read ...

You will have to read these six books for your dog as well as yourself. You will be both student and teacher. A dog is a fine student—*if* you are a fine teacher!

Your dog will supply his talent to learn. He will work for praise, play, and treats because they create safety, happiness, and comfort.

In this book, you will learn how to speak to an animal that does not know your language. Be patient. Teach one word at a time. Be encouraging. The more you can speak to your dog, the more you can share in the good life of being companions!

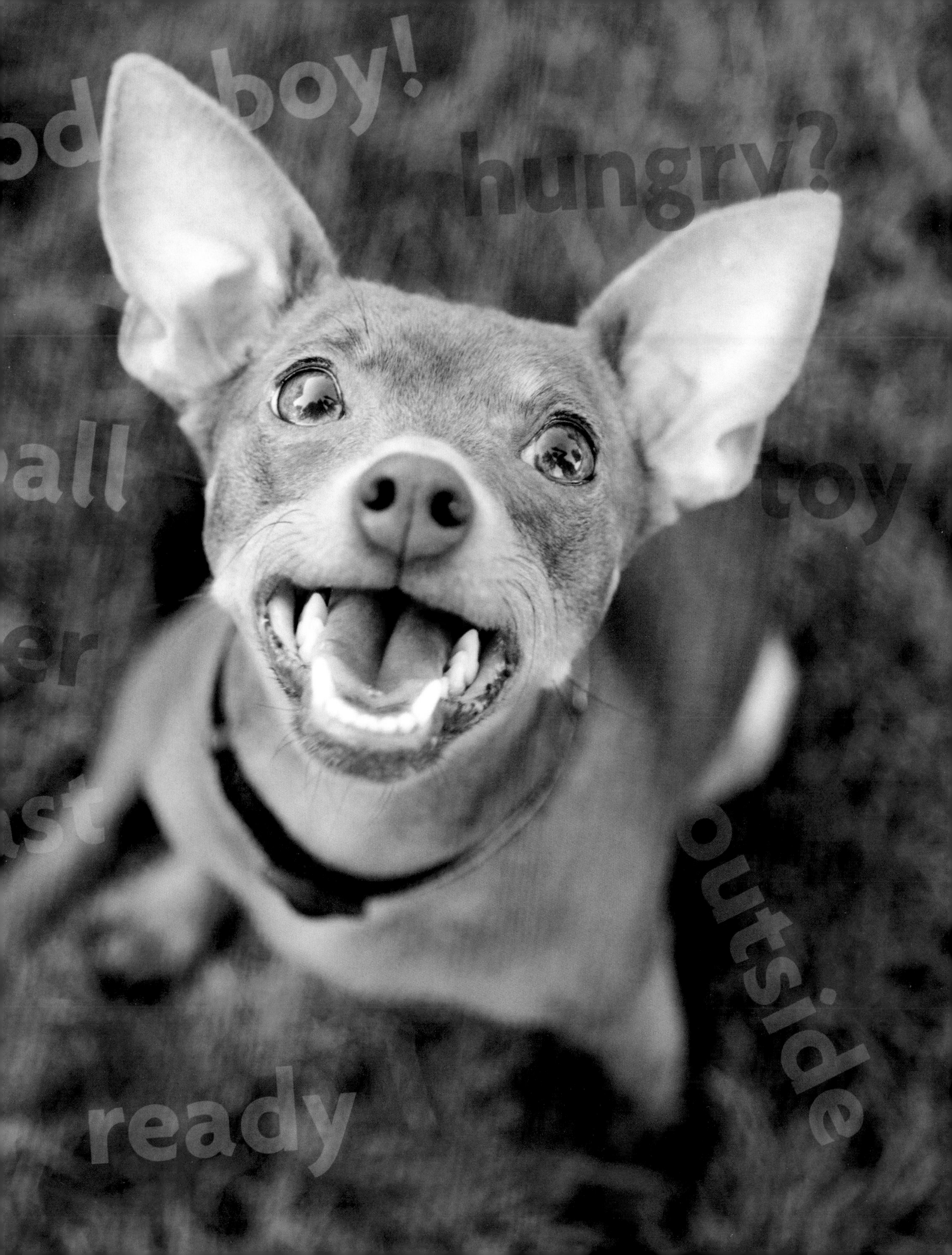
boy!
hungry?
toy
outside
ready

Train Your Voice

Most commands are spoken seriously but not angrily. Cheerfully say your dog's name, and then state the command—SIT, DOWN, or HEEL. Never yell, whine, or giggle when giving a command.

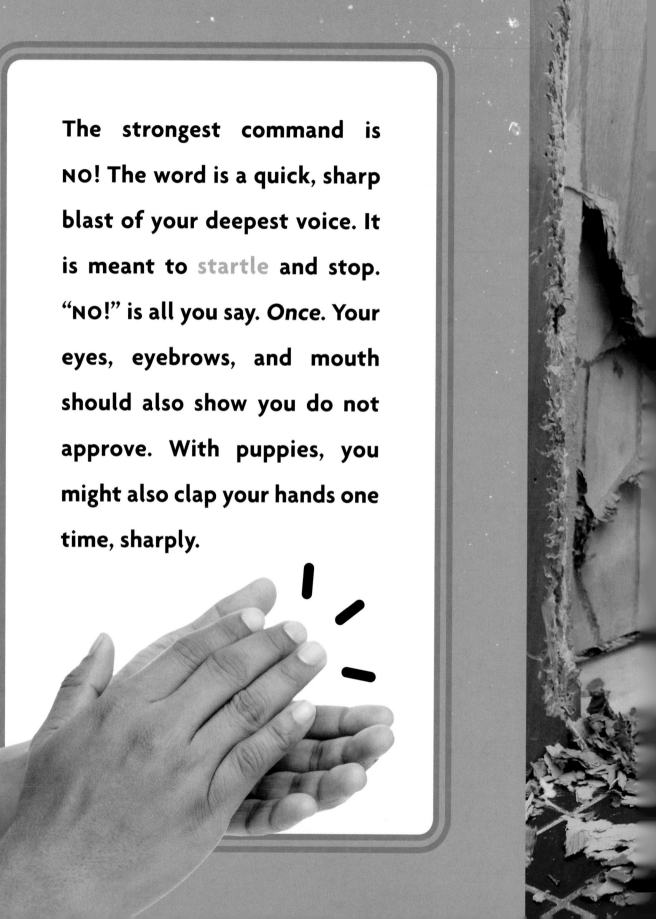

The strongest command is NO! The word is a quick, sharp blast of your deepest voice. It is meant to startle and stop. "NO!" is all you say. *Once.* Your eyes, eyebrows, and mouth should also show you do not approve. With puppies, you might also clap your hands one time, sharply.

The COME command is the opposite of NO. Be encouraging and excited. An anxious or nervous dog needs calming words. Reassure your dog by speaking softly, slowly, and calmly.

Praises should sparkle. Make your words chirpy, lively, and musical. *"Who's the best dog ever? Such a good boy!"*

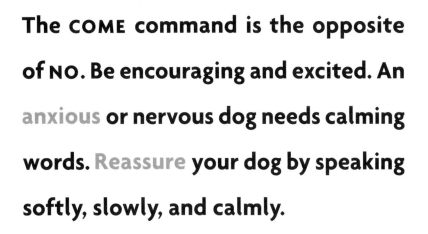

Sing Your Praises

A dog's ears will pick up all your cheerful and loving words! But dogs also experience praise in other ways.

Pat the dog, rub him behind the ears, scratch his chest, let him lick you.

Make eye contact. Smile and lower yourself to the dog's level. This shows trust.

A quick chase, short tussle, tug on a toy, or round of fetch can also be a reward.

Treats are praise as well. Just limit the number your dog gets each day.

Canine Word Power

How do you teach your dog new words? For actions he does naturally—shake off, drink, jump—say the word each time the dog does just that. Say "SHAKE" when your dog is wet and shakes his fur.

Use the same word for each action, object, or place. Say "STEPS" and point to the steps where you want the dog to wait. Add a hand signal. Touch the step. Look at that spot. Say "STEPS" (just once). If the dog reacts, praise him!

BASIC COMMANDS

sit

down

stay

wait

watch me

leave it

shake paws

catch

kiss

bye-bye

find it!

speak

quiet

Answering Questions

Call each toy by the same name every time. Repeat the toy's name while the dog is playing with it. "*RING? Want to play with your RING? Get the RING!*"

Can dogs answer questions? Try sliding your voice upward at the end of your question, and see what happens.

"Where's your BALL?" "Ready for a WALK?" Learning to speak to your dog "unleashes" more ways that you can share time together!

Find It!

This game uses your dog's natural scenting abilities.

▶ Rub your hands on a treat or toy. Show it to your dog. Command him to SIT/STAY, or have a friend hold the dog on a leash.

▶ Walk away and "hide" the treat or toy where your dog can see it.

▶ Say "OKAY" and then "FIND IT!" When the dog gets it, offer praise.

▶ **Repeat a few more times. Hide the toy farther away, in a different room, underneath or inside something. If your dog loses interest, encourage him. If he cannot find it quickly, you find it, act excited, and give it to your dog.**

Glossary

anxious: restless, nervous, or worried; an anxious dog will often whine or pant

encouraging: giving support and advice

patient: calm and peaceful, not angry or upset

reassure: make someone feel less afraid or upset

signal: a motion used to produce a specific action

startle: to cause a sudden feeling of shock or alarm

Websites

American Kennel Club: Dog Training Basics
http://www.akc.org/content/dog-training/basics/
Pick up tips for training your dog.

Ducksters: Dogs
http://www.ducksters.com/animals/dogs.php
Find out how to choose the right kind of dog for you.

Index

Note: Every effort has been made to ensure that the websites listed above are suitable for children, that they have educational value, and that they contain no inappropriate material. However, because of the nature of the Internet, it is impossible to guarantee that these sites will remain active indefinitely or that their contents will not be altered.